KU-739-424

The Usborne Little Book of

Christmas Carols

Illustrated by
Stephen Cartwright

Designed by Amanda Gulliver

Contents

3

Away in a manger

1 Away in a manger, no crib for a bed,
The little Lord Jesus lay down his sweet head,
The stars in the bright sky looked down where he lay,
The little Lord Jesus asleep on the hay.

2 The cattle are lowing, the baby awakes,
But little Lord Jesus, no crying he makes.
I love thee, Lord Jesus! Look down from the sky,
And stay by my side until morning is nigh.

3 Be near me Lord Jesus; I ask thee to stay
Close by me for ever and love me, I pray.
Bless all the dear children in thy tender care,
And fit us for heaven to live with thee there.

The holly
and the ivy

1 The holly and the ivy,
When they are both full grown,
Of all the trees that are in the wood,
The holly bears the crown.

0 the rising of the sun,
And the running of the deer,
The playing of the merry organ,
Sweet singing in the choir.

2 The holly bears a blossom,
As white as any flower,
And Mary bore sweet Jesus Christ,
To be our sweet Saviour:

0 the rising of the sun. . .

3 The holly bears a berry,
   As red as any blood,
And Mary bore sweet Jesus Christ,
   To do poor sinners good.

0 the rising of the sun. . .

4 The holly bears a prickle,
   As sharp as any thorn,
And Mary bore sweet Jesus Christ,
   On Christmas Day in the morn.

0 the rising of the sun. . .

5 The holly bears a bark,
   As bitter as any gall,
And Mary bore sweet Jesus Christ,
   For to redeem us all.

0 the rising of the sun. . .

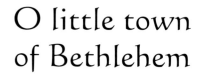

O little town of Bethlehem

1 O little town of Bethlehem,
How still we see thee lie.
Above thy deep and dreamless sleep,
The silent stars go by.
Yet in thy dark streets shineth
The everlasting light.
The hopes and fears of all the years
Are met in thee tonight.

2 O morning stars together
Proclaim thy holy birth.
And praises sing to God the King
And peace to men on Earth.
For Christ is born of Mary
And, gathered all above
While mortals sleep, the angels keep
Their watch of wondering love.

3 How silently, how silently,
The wondrous gift is given.
So God imparts to human hearts
The blessings of his Heaven.
No ear may hear his coming,
But in this world of sin,
Where meek souls will receive him, still
The dear Christ enters in.

4 O holy child of Bethlehem,
Descend to us we pray.
Cast out our sin, and enter in,
Be born in us today.
We hear the Christmas angels
The great glad tidings tell:
O come to us, abide with us,
Our Lord Emmanuel.

Ding dong! Merrily on high

1 Ding dong! Merrily on high, in Heaven the bells are ringing,
Ding dong! Verily the sky is riven with angels singing.

Gloria, hosanna in excelsis.
Gloria, hosanna in excelsis.

2 And on earth below, below, let steeple bells be swungen,
And i-o, i-o, i-o, by priest and people sungen.

Gloria, hosanna in excelsis.
Gloria, hosanna in excelsis.

3 Pray you dutifully prime your matin chime, you ringers,
May you beautifully rhyme your eve-time song, you singers.

Gloria, hosanna in excelsis.
Gloria, hosanna in excelsis.

12

The first nowell

1 The first nowell the angel did say,
Was to certain poor shepherds in fields as they lay;
In fields where they lay keeping their sheep,
On a cold winter's night that was so deep.

Nowell, nowell, nowell, nowell,
Born is the King of Israel.

2 They looked up and saw a star,
Shining in the east, beyond them far.
And to the Earth it gave great light,
And so it continued both day and night.

Nowell, nowell, nowell, nowell. . .

3 And by the light of that same star,
Three wise men came from country far;
To seek for a King was their intent,
And to follow the star wherever it went.

Nowell, nowell, nowell, nowell. . .

4 This star drew nigh unto the north-west,
  O'er Bethlehem it took its rest.
  And there it did both stop and stay,
  Right over the place where Jesus lay.

Nowell, nowell, nowell, nowell. . .

5 Then entered in those wise men three,
  Full reverently upon their knee,
  And offered there, in his presence,
  Their gold and myrrh and frankincense.

Nowell, nowell, nowell, nowell. . .

6 Then let us all with one accord,
  Sing praises to our heavenly Lord,
  That hath made Heaven and Earth of nought,
  And with his blood mankind hath bought.

Nowell, nowell, nowell, nowell. . .

Unto us a child is born

1 Unto us a child is born!
King of all creation.
Came into a world forlorn,
The Lord of every nation.

2 Cradled in a stall was he
With sleepy cows and asses;
But the very beasts could see
That he all men surpasses.

3 Herod then with fear was filled:
"A prince," he said, "in Jewry!"
  All the little boys he killed
  At Bethlehem in his fury.

4 Now may Mary's son, who came
    So long ago to love us,
  Lead us all with hearts aflame
  Unto the joys above us.

5 Omega and Alpha he!
    Let the organ thunder,
While the choir with peals of glee,
  Doth rend the air asunder.

It came upon the midnight clear

1 It came upon the midnight clear,
   That glorious song of old,
From angels bending near the Earth,
   To touch their harps of gold:
"Peace on the Earth, good will to men,
   From Heaven's all-gracious King,"
The world in solemn stillness lay
   To hear the angels sing.

2 Still through the cloven skies they come,
   With peaceful wings unfurled,
And still their heavenly music floats
   O'er all the weary world;
Above its sad and lowly plains
   They bend on heavenly wing,
And ever o'er its Babel-sounds
   The blessed angels sing.

3 Yet with the woes of sin and strife,
The world has suffered long.
Beneath the angel-strain have rolled
Two thousand years of wrong.
And man, at war with man, hears not
The love song which they bring.
Oh, hush the noise, ye men of strife,
And hear the angels sing!

4 For lo! the days are hastening on,
By prophet-bards foretold,
When with the ever-circling years
Comes round the age of gold:
When peace shall over all the Earth
Its ancient splendours fling,
And the whole world send back the song
Which now the angels sing.

Good Christian men, rejoice!

1 Good Christian men, rejoice!
With heart and soul and voice!
Give ye heed to what we say,
Jesus Christ is born today.
Ox and ass before him bow,
And he is in the manger now.
Christ is born today!
Christ is born today!

2 Good Christian men, rejoice!
With heart and soul and voice!
Now ye hear of endless bliss:
Jesus Christ was born for this.
He hath ope'd the heavenly door,
And man is blessed for ever more.
Christ was born for this!
Christ was born for this!

3 Good Christian men, rejoice!
With heart and soul and voice!
Now ye need not fear the grave
Jesus Christ was born to save!
Calls you one and calls you all,
To gain his everlasting hall.
Christ was born to save!
Christ was born to save!

Angels from the realms of glory

1 Angels from the realms of glory,
Wing your flight o'er all the Earth;
Ye who sang creation's story
Now proclaim Messiah's birth:
Gloria in excelsis Deo.
Gloria in excelsis Deo.

2 Shepherds in the field abiding,
Watching o'er your flocks by night,
God with man is now residing;
Yonder shines the infant light:
Gloria in excelsis Deo...

3 Sages, leave your contemplations,
   Brighter visions beam afar.
Seek the great desire of nations,
   Ye have seen his natal star:
   Gloria in excelsis Deo...

4 Saints before the altar bending,
   Watching long in hope and fear,
Suddenly the Lord, descending,
   In his temple shall appear:
   Gloria in excelsis Deo...

5 Though an infant now we view him,
   He shall fill his Father's throne,
Gather all the nations round him,
   Every knee shall then bow down:
   Gloria in excelsis Deo...

21

Silent night

1 Silent night, holy night,
All is calm, all is bright,
All around the mother and child,
Holy infant so tender and mild,
Sleep in heavenly peace,
Sleep in heavenly peace.

2 Silent night, holy night,
Shepherds wake at the sight.
Glory streams from heaven afar,
Heavenly hosts sing Alleluia.
Christ the Saviour is born!
Christ the Saviour is born!

3 Silent night, holy night,
Son of God, love's pure light;
Radiance beams from thy holy face,
With the dawn of redeeming grace,
Jesus, Lord at thy birth,
Jesus, Lord at thy birth.

See amid the winter's snow

1 See amid the winter's snow,
Born for us on Earth below:
See the tender Lamb appears,
Promised from eternal years.

Hail, thou ever-blessed morn;
Hail, redemption's happy dawn;
Sing through all Jerusalem,
Christ is born in Bethlehem.

2 Lo, within a manger lies,
He who built the starry skies
He who, throned in height sublime,
Sits amid the cherubim.

Hail, thou ever-blessed morn. . .

3 Say, ye holy shepherds, say,
What your joyful news today;
Wherefore have ye left your sheep
On the lonely mountain steep?

Hail, thou ever-blessed morn. . .

4 "As we watched at dead of night,
   Lo, we saw a wondrous light;
   Angels singing peace on Earth,
   Told us of the Saviour's birth."

Hail, thou ever-blessed morn. . .

5 Sacred Infant, all divine,
What a tender love was thine,
Thus to come from highest bliss
Down to such a world as this!

Hail, thou ever-blessed morn. . .

6 Teach, oh teach us, Holy Child,
   By thy face so meek and mild.
   Teach us to resemble thee
   In thy sweet humility.

Hail, thou ever-blessed morn. . .

The birds

1 From out of a wood did a cuckoo fly,
Cuckoo.
He came to a manger with joyful cry,
Cuckoo.
He hopped, he curtsied, round he flew,
And loud his jubilation grew,
Cuckoo, cuckoo, cuckoo.

2 A pigeon flew over to Galilee,
Vrercroo.
He strutted and cooed, and was full of glee,
Vrercroo.
And showed with jewelled wings unfurled,
His joy that Christ was in the world,
Vrercroo, vrercroo, vrercroo.

3 A dove settled down upon Nazareth,
Tsucroo.
And tenderly chanted with all his breath
Tsucroo:
"O you," he cooed, "so good and true,
My beauty do I give to you."
Tsucroo, tsucroo, tsucroo.

Gabriel's message

1 The angel Gabriel from heaven came,
His wings as drifted snow, his eyes as flame.
"All hail," he said, "thou lowly maiden Mary,
Most highly favoured lady,"
Gloria!

2 "For known a blessed Mother thou shalt be,
All generations laud and honour thee,
Thy son shall be Emmanuel, by seers foretold.
Most highly favoured lady,"
Gloria!

3 Then gentle Mary meekly bowed her head,
 "To me be as it pleaseth God," she said,
"My soul shall laud and magnify his holy name."
Most highly favoured lady,
Gloria!

4 Of her, Emmanuel, the Christ, was born
In Bethlehem, all on a Christmas morn,
And Christian folk throughout the world will ever say:
"Most highly favoured lady,"
Gloria!

Hark! the herald angels sing

1 Hark! the herald angels sing,
Glory to the newborn King.
Peace on Earth, and mercy mild,
God and sinners reconciled.
Joyful, all you nations rise,
Join the triumph of the skies.
With the angelic hosts proclaim,
"Christ is born in Bethlehem."

Hark! the herald angels sing,
"Glory to the newborn King."

2 Christ, by highest Heaven adored,
    Christ, the everlasting Lord.
    Late in time behold him come,
    Offspring of a virgin's womb.
    Veiled in flesh the Godhead see;
    Hail, the incarnate Deity,
    Pleased as man with man to dwell,
    Jesus, our Emmanuel!

Hark! the herald angels sing,
"Glory to the newborn King."

3 Hail, the Heaven-born Prince of Peace!
    Hail, the Sun of Righteousness!
    Light and life to all he brings,
    Risen with healing in his wings.
    Mild he lays his glory by,
    Born that man no more may die,
    Born to raise the sons of Earth,
    Born to give them second birth.

Hark! the herald angels sing,
"Glory to the newborn King."

In the bleak midwinter

1 In the bleak midwinter
Frosty wind made moan,
Earth stood hard as iron,
Water like a stone;
Snow had fallen, snow on snow,
Snow on snow,
In the bleak midwinter,
Long ago.

2 Our God, Heaven cannot hold him
Nor Earth sustain;
Heaven and Earth shall flee away
When he comes to reign.
In the bleak midwinter
A stable place sufficed
The Lord God Almighty
Jesus Christ.

3 Enough for him whom cherubim
Worship night and day
A breastful of milk
And a mangerful of hay;
Enough for him, whom angels
Fall down before,
The ox and ass and camel
Which adore.

4 Angels and archangels
May have gathered there,
Cherubim and seraphim
Thronged the air,
But only his mother
In her maiden bliss
Worshipped the beloved
With a kiss.

5 What can I give him
Poor as I am?
If I were a shepherd
I would bring a lamb;
If I were a wise man
I would do my part
Yet what I can I give him
Give my heart.

The Coventry carol

1 Lully, lulla, thou little tiny child,
    By, by, lully, lullay,
    Lully, thou little tiny child,
    By, by, lully, lullay.

2 O sisters too, how may we do,
    For to preserve this day,
    This poor youngling for whom we do sing,
    By, by, lully, lullay.

3 Herod the king in his raging,
Charged he hath this day
His men of might, in his own sight,
All children young to slay.

4 Then woe is me, poor child, for thee
And ever mourn and say,
For thy parting nor say nor sing,
By, by, lully, lullay.

O come, all ye faithful

1 O come, all ye faithful,
Joyful and triumphant,
O come ye, O come ye to Bethlehem.
Come and behold him,
Born the King of Angels,

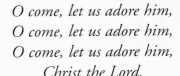

O come, let us adore him,
O come, let us adore him,
O come, let us adore him,
Christ the Lord.

2 God of God
Light of Light,
Lo! He abhors not the Virgin's womb;
Very God,
Begotten, not created:

O come, let us adore him. . .

3 Sing, choirs of angels,
Sing in exultation,
Sing, all you citizens of Heaven above;
Glory to God
In the highest:

O come, let us adore him. . .

4 Yea, Lord, we greet thee,
Born this happy morning,
Jesus, to thee be glory given;
Word of the Father,
Now in flesh appearing:

O come, let us adore him. . .

O come, O come, Emmanuel!

1 O come, O come, Emmanuel!
Redeem thy captive Israel,
That into exile drear is gone
Far from the face of God's dear son.

Rejoice! Rejoice! Emmanuel
Shall come to thee, O Israel.

2 O come, thou branch of Jesse! draw
The quarry from the lion's claw;
From the dread caverns of the grave,
From nether hell, thy people save.

Rejoice! Rejoice! Emmanuel
Shall come to thee, O Israel.

3 O come, O come, thou dayspring bright!
  Pour on our souls thy healing light;
Dispel the long night's lingering gloom,
  And pierce the shadows of the tomb.

  Rejoice! Rejoice! Emmanuel
  Shall come to thee, O Israel.

4 O come, thou lord of David's key!
  The royal door fling wide and free;
Safeguard for us the heavenward road,
  And bar the way to death's abode.

  Rejoice! Rejoice! Emmanuel
  Shall come to thee, O Israel.

5 O come, O come, Adonai,
  Who in thy glorious majesty
From that high mountain clothed with awe
  Gavest thy folk the elder law.

  Rejoice! Rejoice! Emmanuel
  Shall come to thee, O Israel.

We three kings of Orient are

1 We three kings of Orient are,
Bearing gifts we travel so far,
Field and fountain, moor and mountain,
Following yonder star.

O star of wonder, star of night,
Star with royal beauty bright,
Westward leading, still proceeding,
Guide us to thy perfect light.

2 Born a king on Bethlehem's plain,
Gold I bring, to crown him again,
King forever, ceasing never,
Over us all to reign.

O star of wonder, star of night...

3 Frankincense to offer have I,
Incense owns a Deity nigh.
Prayer and praising, all men raising
Worshipping God most high.

O star of wonder, star of night...

4 Myrrh is mine, its bitter perfume
Breathes a life of gathering gloom;
Sorrowing, sighing, bleeding, dying,
Sealed in the stone-cold tomb.

O star of wonder, star of night...

5 Glorious now behold him arise,
King and God and sacrifice,
Alleluia, Alleluia;
Earth to the heavens replies.

O star of wonder, star of night...

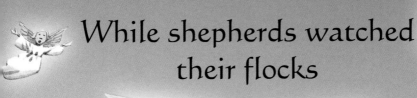

While shepherds watched their flocks

1 While shepherds watched their flocks by night,
   All seated on the ground,
   The angel of the Lord came down,
   And glory shone around.

2 "Fear not," said he, for mighty dread
   Had seized their troubled mind;
   "Glad tidings of great joy I bring
   To you and all mankind.

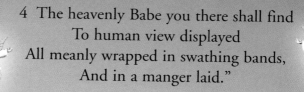

3 To you in David's town this day
　　Is born of David's line
A Saviour, who is Christ the Lord,
　　And this shall be the sign:

4 The heavenly Babe you there shall find
　　To human view displayed
All meanly wrapped in swathing bands,
　　And in a manger laid."

5 Thus spake the seraph; and forthwith
　　Appeared a shining throng
Of angels praising God, who thus
　　Addressed their joyful song:

6 "All glory be to God on high,
　　And to the Earth be peace;
Goodwill henceforth from Heaven to men
　　Begin and never cease."

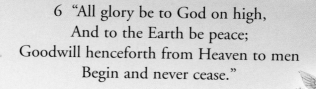

Once in royal David's city

1 Once in royal David's city
Stood a lowly cattle shed,
Where a mother laid her baby,
In a manger for his bed.
Mary was that mother mild,
Jesus Christ her little child.

2 He came down to Earth from Heaven
Who is God and Lord of all,
And his shelter was a stable,
And his cradle was a stall.
With the poor and mean and lowly
Lived on Earth our Saviour holy.

3 And through all his wondrous childhood
He would honour and obey,
Love and watch the lowly maiden,
In whose gentle arms he lay.
Christian children all must be,
Mild, obedient, good as he.

4 For he is our childhood's pattern,
 Day by day like us he grew,
He was little, weak and helpless,
Tears and smiles like us he knew,
And he feeleth for our sadness,
And he shareth in our gladness.

5 And our eyes at last shall see him,
Through his own redeeming love,
For that child so dear and gentle
 Is our Lord in Heaven above,
And he leads his children on
To the place where he is gone.

6 Not in that poor lowly stable,
 With the oxen standing by,
We shall see him, but in Heaven
Set at God's right hand on high,
Where, like stars, his children crowned
All in white shall wait around.

45

How far is it to Bethlehem?

1 How far is it to Bethlehem?
Not very far.
Shall we find a stable room
Lit by a star?
Can we see the little child,
Is he within?
If we lift the wooden latch,
May we go in?

2 May we stroke the creatures there
Ox, ass or sheep?
May we peep like them and see
Jesus asleep?
If we touch his tiny hand
Will he awake?
Will he know we've come so far
Just for his sake?

3 Great kings have precious gifts,
And we have naught.
Little smiles and little tears are
All we brought.
For all weary children
Mary must weep,
Here on his bed of straw,
Sleep, children, sleep.

Good King Wenceslas

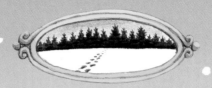

1 Good King Wenceslas looked out
On the feast of Stephen,
When the snow lay round about
Deep and crisp and even.
Brightly shone the moon that night,
Though the frost was cruel,
When a poor man came in sight,
Gathering winter fuel.

2 "Hither, page and stand by me,
If you know it, telling,
Yonder peasant, who is he?
Where and what his dwelling?"
"Sire, he lives a good league hence,
Underneath the mountain,
Right against the forest fence,
By St. Agnes' fountain."

3 "Bring me flesh and bring me wine,
    Bring me pine-logs hither.
   You and I will see him dine.
   When we bear them thither."
 Page and monarch, forth they went,
    Forth they went together,
 Through the rude wind's wild lament
    And the bitter weather.

4 "Sire, the night is darker now.
    And the wind blows stronger;
   Fails my heart, I know not how;
    I can go no longer."
 "Mark my footsteps, good my page;
    Tread thou in them boldly:
   Thou shalt find the winter's rage
    Freeze thy blood less coldly."

5 In his master's steps he trod,
    Where the snow lay dinted;
   Heat was in the very sod
    Which the saint had printed.
 Therefore, Christian men, be sure,
    Wealth or rank possessing,
   Ye who now will bless the poor,
    Shall yourselves find blessing.

God rest you merry gentlemen

1 God rest you merry gentlemen,
Let nothing you dismay,
For Jesus Christ our Saviour
Was born on Christmas Day;
To save us all from Satan's power
When we had gone astray.

O tidings of comfort and joy,
Comfort and joy,
O tidings of comfort and joy.

2 In Bethlehem in Jewry
This blessed babe was born,
And laid within a manger
Upon this blessed morn;
Which his good mother Mary
Did nothing take in scorn.

O tidings of comfort and joy. . .

3 From God, our heavenly Father,
   A blessed angel came,
   And unto certain shepherds
   Brought tidings of the same,
   That there was born in Bethlehem
   The Son of God by name.

      O tidings of comfort and joy. . .

4 But when they came to Bethlehem
   Where our dear Saviour lay,
   They found him in a manger,
   Where oxen feed on hay;
   His mother, Mary, kneeling,
   Unto the Lord did pray.

   O tidings of comfort and joy. . .

5 Now to the Lord sing praises,
   All you within this place,
   And with true love and brotherhood
   Each other now embrace;
   This holy tide of Christmas
   All others doth deface.

      O tidings of comfort and joy. . .

51

Here we come a-wassailing

1 Here we come a-wassailing,
   Among the leaves so green.
   Here we come a-wandering,
   So fair to be seen.

Love and joy come to you
And to you your wassail too
And God bless you, and send you
A happy New Year,
And God send you a happy New Year.

2 Our wassail cup is made
   Of the rosemary tree,
   And so is your beer
   Of the best barley.

Love and joy come to you. . .

3 We are not daily beggars
That beg from door to door,
But we are neighbours' children
Whom you have seen before.

Love and joy come to you...

4 Bring us out a table,
And spread it with a cloth;
Bring us out a mouldy cheese,
And some of your Christmas loaf.

Love and joy come to you...

God bless the master of this house;
Likewise the mistress too;
And all the little children
That round the table go.

Love and joy come to you...

Past three o'clock

Past three o'clock,
And a cold frosty morning;
Past three o'clock,
Good morrow, masters all.

1 Born is a baby,
  Gentle as may be,
  Son of the eternal
  Father supernal.

Past three o'clock. . .

2 Seraph choir singeth,
  Angel bell ringeth;
  Hark how they rhyme it,
  Time it and chime it.

Past three o'clock. . .

3 Mid earth rejoices,
  Hearing such voices,
  Ne'ertofore so well
  Carolling nowell.

Past three o'clock. . .

4 Hinds o'er the pearly,
  Dewy lawn early,
  Seek the high stranger
  Laid in the manger.

Past three o'clock. . .

5 Cheese from the dairy,
   Bring they for Mary,
   And, not for money,
   Butter and honey.

   Past three o'clock. . .

6 Light out of star-land
   Leadeth from far land
   Princes, to meet him,
   Worship and greet him.

   Past three o'clock. . .

7 Myrrh from the coffer,
   Incense they offer:
   Nor is the golden
   Nugget withholden.

   Past three o'clock. . .

8 Thus they: I pray you,
   Up, sirs, nor stay you
   Till ye confess him
   Likewise, and bless him.

   Past three o'clock. . .

The twelve days of Christmas

On the first day of Christmas, my true love gave to me
A partridge in a pear tree.

On the second day of Christmas, my true love gave to me
Two turtle doves, and a partridge in a pear tree.

On the third day of Christmas, my true love gave to me
Three French hens, two turtle doves,
and a partridge in a pear tree.

On the fourth day of Christmas, my true love gave to me
Four colly birds, three French hens, two turtle doves,
and a partridge in a pear tree.

On the fifth day of Christmas, my true love gave to me
Five gold rings, four colly birds, three French hens,
two turtle doves and a partridge in a pear tree.

On the sixth day of Christmas, my true love gave to me
Six geese a-laying, five gold rings. . .

On the seventh day of Christmas, my true love gave to me
Seven swans a-swimming, six geese a-laying. . .

On the eighth day of Christmas, my true love gave to me
Eight maids a-milking, seven swans a-swimming. . .

On the ninth day of Christmas, my true love gave to me
Nine ladies dancing, eight maids a-milking. . .

On the tenth day of Christmas, my true love gave to me
Ten lords a-leaping, nine ladies dancing. . .

On the eleventh day of Christmas, my true love gave to me
Eleven pipers piping, ten lords a-leaping. . .

On the twelfth day of Christmas, my true love gave to me
Twelve drummers drumming, eleven pipers piping. . .

Deck the hall with boughs of holly

1 Deck the hall with boughs of holly,
    Fa la la la la, la la la la,
    'Tis the season to be jolly,
    Fa la la la la, la la la la,
    Don we now our gay apparel,
    Fa la la, la la la, la la la,
    Troll the ancient Yuletide carol,
    Fa la la la la, la la la la.

2 See the blazing Yule before us,
Fa la la la la, la la la la,
Strike the harp and join the chorus,
Fa la la la la, la la la la,
Follow me in merry measure,
Fa la la, la la la, la la la,
While I tell of Yuletide treasure,
Fa la la la la, la la la la.

3 Fast away the old year passes,
Fa la la la la, la la la la,
Hail the new, ye lads and lasses,
Fa la la la la, la la la la,
Sing we joyous all together,
Fa la la, la la la, la la la,
Heedless of the wind and weather,
Fa la la la la, la la la la.

We wish you a merry Christmas

1 We wish you a merry Christmas,
We wish you a merry Christmas,
We wish you a merry Christmas,
And a happy new year.

Good tidings we bring
To you and your kin;
We wish you a merry Christmas
And a happy new year.

2 We all want some figgy pudding,
We all want some figgy pudding,
We all want some figgy pudding,
So bring some right here!

Good tidings we bring. . .

3 We won't go until we get some,
We won't go until we get some,
We won't go until we get some,
So bring some right here!

Good tidings we bring. . .

Index of first lines